CW01560903

About the Author

Teri started writing poetry at the age of ten. At seventeen she adopted the nom-de-plume of Teri O'Neal. She was an active writer and performer of her work through to her early thirties, at which point she met her husband and life-partner, and, for various reasons, virtually stopped writing. However, she always knew that it was still there and she would go back to it if he was no longer in her life. He died suddenly of a heart attack, their having been together for over forty years. Twelve days later she started writing again and continues to do so. Professionally, she worked as a corporate treasurer for over thirty years. She is also an artist (as Teri Walsh), working primarily in the medium of screen printing.

* Photograph by Jane de Weck Photography

You are dead (but I am not...)
[or A Diary of Grief]

Teri O'Neal

You are dead (but I am not...)
[or A Diary of Grief]

Olympia Publishers
London

www.olympiapublishers.com

OLYMPIA PAPERBACK EDITION

Cover by Teri O'Neal

Copyright © Teri O'Neal 2025

A CIP catalogue record for this title is
available from the British Library.

ISBN: 978-1-83543-247-1

This book is a memoir in poetic form. It reflects the author's
experiences and recollections at the time of the events. Some names
or characteristics have been changed, some events have been
compressed, and some dialogue has been recreated.

First Published in 2025

Olympia Publishers
Tallis House
2 Tallis Street
London
EC4Y 0AB

Printed in Great Britain

Dedication

I dedicate this book to my late husband Patrick. Thank you for everything.

Acknowledgements

Thank you to all my friends who have supported and
encouraged me both in my grief and in writing these poems.
You know who you are! Thank you.

Contents

Empty

How are you feeling?
Nothing
I feel nothing
Numb
Empty

There's an empty side of the bed
The cat shoves me over
And I occupy the empty side of the bed
And it is still
Empty

06/12/21

I always said

I always said
That if you went first
I would decide whether or not
I wanted to continue

Now that you have gone
I can't make up my mind

07/12/21

Coincidences

CO-

    IN-

        CID-

            ENCES

I don't believe in coincidence

So no you didn't bring me an Advent calendar
As a gift
The first I have ever had in my life
And it didn't have little chocolate hearts in it
And I didn't open one each day of Advent
And this wasn't after you died

And no
The lady who looked after our cat when we were away
Didn't die on the same day
Also of a heart attack

And no
The day of your death was not the
42nd anniversary of the day we met

And no
When I went up onto the Downs
For the first time in months
I didn't go to see "your bench" at the Dew Pond
And no it wasn't strewn with masses of
Your favourite flowers

In memory?
Of whom?

02/01/22

The second stage?

They say that anger
     is
            the second stage
of
     grief

Within a couple of
      minutes
I was shouting

HOW COULD YOU DO THIS TO ME?!

And was very foot-stampingly
Angry
    with
        you

03/01/22

T O'N

Teri O'Neal says "I'm back.
I was never very far away"

It wasn't much of a sacrifice
            if sacrifice at all
To send her away
To not be her

In exchange
        for
                forty-two years

of happiness

                                        15/01/22

What's in a name?
(Coincidences 2)

Nora   Nora

I have only met two Noras
One was my mother's
                    beloved carer
The other was the Staff Nurse
                    who held her hand
                        as she died

Pat(rick)   Pat(ricia)

I have known lots of Pats
I am the widow of one
She is the widow of
                my first husband

[and I was with another Pat(ricia) when I wrote this]

24/01/22

The question

How are you feeling?

    How are you feeling?

        How are you feeling?

That question
Over & over again

But it is
    of course
        the only question

The only one that matters

But the answer?
    I don't know how I feel
        I don't think I feel anything

Maybe the answer is
    nothing

Just emptiness
    nothingness

25/01/22

I felt different

I felt different
　　　for a little while

A Saturday morning

The sun was shining
　　　it was chilly
　　　　　but not too windy

A walk down the hill
　　　to the post office
　　　　　and then on to Waitrose

A spring in my step
　　　I enjoyed it
　　　　　I felt something

For a little while

It didn't last

The weather changed
　　　grey and wet and miserable
　　　　　again

So did my mood
Nothingness returned

07/02/22

I stood there

I stood there
    in my new black flared coat
        with a little black bow / pillbox
           on my head
      [You would have loved the outfit]
And I watched them lower you

Three tears rolled down
    my cheeks
        2 on my left
           1 on the right
My first
    and last
        tears

And I didn't believe
    you were
        in there

And I still don't

                10/02/22

The visit

I visited the grave
        Your grave?
                Our grave
2 days later

To see the flowers

It was heaped thick
        with clay
My message
        had been blown away

The grave next door
        had been disturbed
                almost desecrated

& her headstone put back
        half buried
                crooked

I felt sorry for her family

10/02/22

I don't feel

I don't feel anything
      about
            anything

I just
      am

I just
      exist

I just
      get through
           the days

One by one

So there are less
      left
Before I too
      die

But
      WAIT

This is a
      restart
The start
      of the rest
           of my life

Why do I not
      feel
            excited?

11/02/22

Were you down?

Were you down?
Were you depressed?

I know we had had a
      good weekend
And a really
      nice day

But you were troubled
      by the politics
         the mess of government

By the state of the State

And by health
      your shoulder
         your back
and the cancer
      you had
         survived

Did this contribute
      to the heart attack?

They say it was sudden
      instantaneous
         nothing could have been done

But still doubt
      creeps in
         like a ghost

a big WHAT IF?

A set of WHAT IFS?

And I can't ignore them
can't get rid of them
yet

11/02/22

There but ...

There
        but for the
                grace of God
Go I

I see it in
        their eyes
Friends
        couples for a long time

Look at me
        and think

There
        but
...

20/02/22

Her word

Tall
      thin
            elderly
Smartly dressed
      (Barbour?)

She walked
      into my art show
and we got chatting

It was a difficult
      decision to go ahead
           I say
and explain why

"It happened to me"
she said
Her husband also died
suddenly
in the night
by her side
still,
      cold,
           rigid
when she woke up

"SURREAL"
was her word
Now it is mine

22/02/22

A mini milestone

In two days' time
    it will be three
        months

A quarter of a year
Will have passed

Will have passed
    me by

                        22/02/22

Writing this

These words
These poems

Come
     fully formed

I do not need
     to think
To decide
     what words to use
          what comes next

They just
     are
Are just
     there
          here

(All I have to do is write them down)

25/02/22

Shock

It is a shock
    of a different
        kind
Not
    degree

No time to prepare
No time to discuss
    things
No time to agree
    things
No time to come
    to terms
No time to say
    the things
That should have
    been said

Just
    gone

06/03/22

A friend's word

She saw us together
    a few days before
        you died

Asked me how long we
    had been together

(Over 40 years
    say I)

And she commented
    how vibrant
        our relationship was

What a lovely
    word
        to use
(and so true)

06/03/22

Grief

Is grief
       an illness?

It has symptoms
       stages
              side effects

It is all consuming
       all pervading
but
       separate

07/03/22

I've got to learn

I've got to learn
To say
      my
           and I

Not
    our
        and us

[Please tell me off
    when I get it wrong]

08/03/22

But ...

But
      I am now a
          widow

I have to say it
To tell people
To explain
My change
      of circumstances

Putting a label
      on myself
Defining
      a status
That others understand

I am now a
      widow

13/03/22

Once upon a time

Many decades ago

I wrote about
     other-woman-ness

The idea that being the
     "Other Woman"
conferred
     identity
     status

Now
     I write
        about
widowhood

13/03/22

Another friend's word

She calls it her
  "certainty"
And that certainty
   is their mutual love
The knowledge that they
   will spend their life
     together

You were my certainty
   your belief in me
     your pride
In who I was
In what I did

Sustained and
   supported
     me

Now that has gone
But the memory of it
Sustains and supports me still

          14/03/22

Coincidences (3)

He had travelled a
very long way
To my show
To show
     his support

She had come
from Brighton
With her partner
And their friends
     from London
Who were staying
     with them

Both men were
     physics teachers
Like him
     (although one now writes
          textbooks)

He had met one of them
     before
And had heard of the
     other

I wonder what
     the collective noun
For physics teachers
Is?

14/03/22

I did it

Everyone was surprised
      staggered even
That I could get
      up there
Stand behind the lectern
And read
      a poem
           I had written

Read it there
      at your funeral
Near your coffin
Alongside the family flowers

How did I have
      the strength?
How did I not
      break down?

Don't forget
      I used to perform
Sing
Do poetry readings
Give talks

So I just pressed
      the
           "perform"
Button

15/03/22

A friend rang me

A friend rang me
For a reason

But I just
      jabbered on and on
About all sorts of stuff
All sorts of rubbish

She couldn't get a word
      in edgeways

Eventually she
      managed
To get my attention
To ask me
      to her birthday party

Yes Please!

In future
      people should
         just yell

SHUT UP!

16/03/22

Your day

Today
It's
St Patrick's Day

Your mother always
            sent you a
                        card

She died

So I took over
            the tradition
So that you always
            had
                        one card
On the day

Now
I get reminders
            from the
                        card companies

But
            have no-one
                        to buy one for

17/03/22

Your birthday

It's your birthday
    soon

66
        Clickety
            Click
(the birthday you saw)

67
        Stairway to
            Heaven
(the birthday you didn't reach)

18/03/22

Where's your husband?

Is there somewhere
    quiet
        we can go?

As
    I have something
        to tell you

Do I just say
    that he died
        of a heart attack?

Or do I expose you
    to the full
        horror
Of it all?

19/03/22

Day dreaming

I imagined
      I had gone
            to our favourite
Place
      up on the Downs
And
      sat on your
            bench

And
      cried

26/03/22

One day maybe

A little while
      ago
I was chatting
      to a friend

Her husband
      died
            suddenly
A few years ago

And she didn't
      couldn't
            cry

And then
      one day

She wept
      and wept
            and wept
Until she was
      all cried out

And felt
      better

I hope I can do the same
      one day

26/03/22

Definition

New definition of
     being alone

Having to buy
     your own
          Easter egg

[Waitrose No 1 Hidden Truffles
     Dark Chocolate Easter Egg
          since you ask

And I hadn't read the ingredients properly
     so couldn't eat the truffles
You wouldn't have made that mistake!]

02/04/22

Happy Birthday

It's your birthday
Happy 67th!

I took a taxi
      up to
            Warren Hill

And walked back
      home

Passed the dew pond
Passed your bench
(no flowers here today)
Passed where they collect the
      Ash logs
            before taking them away

Said hello to a lovely
      little white dog
            in its bright red coat
Who jumped up
      and danced around
            in its excitement
(And assured its Mummy that
      that was OK)

Walked down
      alongside the
            A259

Passed the woods

Went diagonally across the
       meadow / green
At the top of the
       road

And came home
       alone

Back to an
       empty house

03/04/22

Preparation

When someone dies
         suddenly
Just like that

You haven't had
         time
To prepare
         yourself

They haven't had
         time
To tidy up
To get rid of stuff
         that's going to leave
                  you
with questions
with doubts

04/04/22

You didn't

I think of you
Talk to you
When watching the
    sport

You didn't:

See Brighton play really
    well
Many times
    and fail to score
        yet again
(but they did win yesterday)

Follow Derby through
    all their trials
        and tribulations
(but Wayne has stuck with them)

See Exeter
    sitting pretty
        in second place
Automatic promotion beckons?
(no more play-off heartache?)

Watch
    when Hamilton
        was robbed
Of a record
    eighth
        title

Hear my
          repeated use of
                    the F word
(definitely not deleted)

Witness the
          spectacle of
                    the abject failure
Of the England team
          in Australia

See England's women
          lose their first three
                    matches
But then win every
          (effectively) knock-out
                    match
To reach the final
          only to be humiliated
                    by Australia

Watch Wales beaten four times including
          by Italy!
England beaten by Scotland
And Ireland only beaten once
          by France
                    the Grand Slam winners

See Sam Waley-Cohen (in his last ride)
Win the Grand National
          (first amateur since 1990)
On Noble Yeats
          (first 7 year old since 1940)

See Tiger Woods

make a comeback
in the Masters
(albeit getting too tired after a very good first round
but at least he made the cut)

10/04/22

TV

You often wondered
What would happen
    if contestants in
        Bargain Hunt
Failed to buy
    three items
Well this couple
    bought only two
(both very cheap – a total of
    only £14 if I remember
        correctly)
And were penalised 75 pounds
(no big spend
    no meeting the
        shopping challenge)
And made a great big
    profit
On the bonus buy
(Charles Hanson
    with one of his really
        expensive items
And this time
    he got it right!)
And the contestants
    took money home

I do quite well at
    Pointless
On my own
    with no team-mate
No-one to confer with

I tried to go back to
        Only Connect
But came to the same
        conclusion
We had reached
Too many questions
        on areas
We knew
        I know
Nothing about
(gaming
        popular culture
                etc.)
So gave up
        again

I watched all of
        Mastermind
And Yes a lot of
        the contestants
                are not very good
These days
But there were a
        number
Who were
        good
And the winner
        was the oldest
                female winner ever
Got 14 out of 14
        on her
                specialist subject
Got a total of
        33 points
                overall

(The highest
        in the series)
And there was a
        tie-break
                in one episode
(the first time for ages)

And I have gone
        back to
Watching MasterChef
        and am
                enjoying it
(but wouldn't want
        to eat
                much of the food)

And then there's
        the sport
But I have already
        up-dated you
                on that

                                15/04/22

Transitioning

That's what I find
        difficult

When to say
        we / our
(the past)

And when to say
        I / mine

(the now)
(the future)

16/04/22

Your do

Well hello
This is your do
I hope I have got
        it right
Understood your instructions
Done what you wanted
Even if I did mess up
        over the date
                forgot the Bank Holiday
(usually you organised major events)

The church?
Well Syd was able
        to organise that
Inigo Jones
        not quite your period but
                wonderful architecture
Which I know you
        admired
And a great location
Very convenient, very central

Why The Garrick?
Well you can blame Syd
        for that too
After all he is
        a Member
Used to take you
        there
And a Gentlemen's' Club
        is very much your

Sort of thing

Champagne?
Well I knew you wouldn't
            forgive me
If we started with
            anything else
(but it is the "House")

Then hot and cold canapes
Mini desserts and coffee

It will be a jolly affair
            and you will be
                        there

18/04/22

What's that noise?
(Coincidences 4)

What's that noise?
Sounds like an
      alarm
I haven't set an
      alarm

Check the radio
      not that
Check the time
      just after midnight
Not been asleep
      very long

Terrible noise
      getting louder
Cat terrified
(cats hear things much louder than humans)

Get up
Think it must be
      the smoke alarm
No smoke
No smell
Check the
      washer dryer
All OK

Still that terrible noise
Dial 999
"Which service

do you want"?
"Sorry to trouble you.
              Am sure there is
                          nothing wrong"
"Which service
              do you want"?

Agree it should be the
              Fire Brigade
"They're on their way
              will be with you very soon"

"Please get out of the house.
              Please take the cat
                          with you"

Don't know how
              I got the cat
                          into her basket

But here we are
              waiting for the
                          Fire Brigade

A man and a woman
Check everywhere
All OK
Just the alarm
              in the attic
Set off by
              spiders / cobwebs
Noise has stopped
Silence!

Then

the three of us
            talking
"Is there anyone else
            in the house"?
"No just me
            and the cat"
Say why
Talk about grief

The man says he understands
            grief
His sister died
            last November
Aged 39
            leaving three young children

Realise he is talking about
Our cat sitter
            who died on the
                        same day as you
The fireman is
            her brother
The one who
            rang me
                        that afternoon

We hug
We have a bond
It is comforting
We are glad
            we have now met

Agree it was
            meant to be

Later (on the phone) his colleague
    says it was a
            privilege to be there
To be a witness

                              20/04/22

Blah, blah, blah

Blah
      Blah
          Blah

(telling someone about
      something
          that has happened
such as
      The Curious Incident of the
          Smoke Alarms in the Night-time)

And then
      I wrote a poem

That seems to be
      my answer
          to everything
These days

20/04/22

The garden

I didn't go out
    into the garden
or even onto
    the patio
or even open
    the French window
for months

But it was Winter
    and that was my
        excuse

The lawns grew
    heartily
Following the Autumn feed
    you had given them
(but not their final cut
    of the year
which you were going
    to do
        when we got back home)
I got someone in
    to do the mowing

But that left the garden
Deadheading
    pruning
        general tidying up

So yesterday and the day before
    it has been

blitzed
Like we used to do
    with the housework
        from time to time
(and I ought to do now)

But there is still
    stuff that needs
        to be done
In the garden
    such as feeding
        watering

And I am able to
    go out there
        now

22/04/22

Cat sitting
(Coincidences 5)

You remember we had a cat sitter
    who died on the
        same day?

Well I needed a new
    cat sitter
        so I could go away
(and be at your Memorial Service)

She is very nice
    and Bella likes her
        and she sends me videos

And she met her husband
    29 years ago
        in the house next door

01/05/22

Grieving

Grieve in your
      own way

Everyone grieves in
      different ways

Do what you feel
Don't worry what other
      people think

The most important
      advice to date
From my doctor
From Pat
On consecutive days

They say I am being brave
      No I'm not
They say I am remarkable
      No I'm not
I'm just being
      Me

Maybe some people
      say
I'm not really
      grieving at all
But I am
But just in
      my own way

08/05/22

Wife / widow

Wife
Widow

Expressions of
      status
Labels

Going from one
      to the other
Should be a
      process
But not if
      sudden

Then it all has to
      happen
Afterwards

I wear my rings
To show I am
      married
But feel there
      is a word
          tattooed
On my forehead
WIDOW

Maybe I should wear
      a black armband

09/05/22

Another milestone

A friend wrote
      to tell me
            that
Soon
      six months
            will have passed

Another milestone

In one sense
      I didn't need
            to be told
In another
      I am grateful
For they will be
      thinking
            of me
And of you
At that time

What next?
      What comes
            after that?
A year?

(But before that
      there is a headstone
            to decide on
To order
To have erected)

                          11/05/22

Flowers

Check-out lady
Checking out my tulips

"I have to buy my own
      flowers
            now"
I say

"So do I
      A house isn't a house
            without flowers"
She replies

13/05/22

That day relived

59 minutes
07:23 to 08:22

The most precious
      59 minutes
           of my life

"You knew"
      - My doctor
"My subconscious knew"
      - Me
"No, YOU knew"

Quiet, peaceful time
Sitting there
Reading my Kindle
No lights on
Silence
Peace
Cold
      so very cold

Yes, I knew

Knew that if I
      put the light on
Saw you
      touched you
I would have to
      face up to it
Seek help

Then (my doctor again)
"The shit would hit the fan"

Unexplained death
A potential crime scene
A suspect
Me

People were very kind
        but I could see the doubts
                in their eyes

Not allowed back
        into our room
Some-one retrieved
        my phone
                my iPad

The police came
        two hours later
(We were not an emergency)

Popped in and out of
        the room I had
                been put in
Asked questions
        Asked the same questions
                Asked new questions
Made notes

Tried to make sense
        of those 59 minutes
I rang people
I emailed people
I had coffee

I had something to eat

A friend arrived
            coming to rescue me
And I gave a formal
            statement
                        to the police
And she was allowed to stay with me
And I checked it
And signed it

And my friend and I
            had a very late
                        light lunch

The police wanted me
            to stay overnight
                        but couldn't make me

But I didn't want my friend
            to do any more driving
Didn't want to leave

But I also didn't want to
            see you again
But my friend / our friend did

She agreed you were
            very peaceful
(almost smiling)

Then dinner
They were deep-cleaning
            our room
I could see over to it

They realised this and
      ran to shut the door
So thoughtful

And they apologised
      they couldn't give me
            a bigger discount
On the two rooms
For the extra night
And they didn't
      charge me for
            food and drinks
From when you died

And the staff all knew
      what had happened
Who I was
      and were caring
            but not gushing

And they sent me
      flowers a week later

And I'll never go back

14/05/22

Today

It's six months
      today

Is today
      the day

the tears start
      to flow

the floodgates
      open

or just another day
      to get through?

24/05/22

The other day

The other day
     (I think it was Monday)
I had had
     my dinner
Drunk my little bit
     of wine
Was watching
     TV
And realised
     I was feeling
          quite content
At peace
At ease
Alone
     but not lonely

Now please don't
     take this
          the wrong way

It
Wasn't that I didn't
     miss you
Wasn't that I didn't
     feel sad
Wasn't that I didn't
     wish you were still here
          with me

But
     at last

I felt

OK

(ish)

04/06/22

Identity

A friend and I
        were talking on the phone
               the other day
About
      identity

I have been thinking
      a lot about this
           recently

"Discussing" it at length
      (by email)
With Pat

Exploring who we both
      now are
Now that we are both
      widows

And my friend said that
      within couples
There are three
      identities:
ME
     YOU
         US

And these are
      quite distinct

And if you are

now on your own
       (for whatever reason)
You have to rescue the
    "ME"

[But a new me]

04/06/22

Preparation (2)

Another topic of
    conversation
        canvassing views / experience

When someone knew that
    their partner
        was dying
How did they prepare?

First you have to accept
    it
Believe it is actually
    going to happen

Then there is timing
    how long?
What to do with the
    time left?

One solution:
    do nice things
Make the most of the
    time
But that time was cut short
    very short

Or another is:
    to be in denial
        buy expensive stereo equipment
Plan for the future

Or yet another is:
      to prepare
My parents were convinced
      (on no evidence)
          that she would go first
So she taught him how
      to cook
Then, knowing he was
      dying
He did not teach her
      anything
So she didn't know
How
      to write a cheque
How
      to get cash from the bank
And I had to take over
And do it all
      for her

But what if
      you don't know
If it is
      unexpected
          sudden?

We had prepared
Put everything in joint names
Agreed how to get rid of stuff
      (The Project)
Expected to have another ten years
      together
But had prepared
But what is the
      common theme

The thing that, in the event,
    takes over

No matter what preparation
    has been undertaken?

SHOCK
Shock
    overwhelms
        everything

        13/06/22

Stages of realisation

Other people's realisation
  comes in stages

My husband is dead
  = you are a widow

You are clearly old
  = you were probably together a long time

It was sudden
  = not cancer, not expected

It was "unexplained"
  = a post mortem

A heart attack
  = no warning (but also no suffering)

It was in the middle of the night
  = did you know at the time? Or
  = was he dead, by your side, when you woke up?
[It was the latter]

We were in a hotel
  = you weren't at home
  = bad

No it equals good
Because we weren't
  in our own bed

Slowly the bits are pieced together
A scenario / sequence of events formed

And
      slowly
           the horror of it all
Crystallises

                          18/06/22

Talking

I find talking to people
      exhausting
I do it so rarely
[other than to you]

And it is usually
      on the phone
            rarely in person

And it tends to be
      in big chunks
          long chats

And it tends to be
      serious
          deep

And it tends to be
      about you
Or about me
      and how I am

And it is usually
      very interesting
And it usually
Helps

But,
      as I say,
         exhausting

20/06/22

The cat

I usually write
In the middle of the night
Having turned on the light

And the cat
      turns over

And stretches out
      taking up even more of the bed

And huffs and
      puffs

And makes it
      very clear

She does NOT
      approve

20/06/22

Thank goodness for ...

Crime novels
Crime series on TV
Police procedurals

So I knew immediately that
        it was
                an "unexplained death"

Knew I couldn't go back
        into the room

Knew the police would
        want to interview me

That they would
        pop in and out
                asking questions
Going over things
Again and again

So
        thank goodness for ...

20/06/22

Your page

I have just heard that
    (finally)
        Prostate Cancer UK
Have closed down your
    Memorial Page

I don't know why this
    mattered so much
        to me
But it did

I wanted to do it
    just before the
        six months' milestone

Anyway its done
And they apologized
    for all the delays
And it raised over
    two thousand pounds
And I know you will be pleased
    with that
And I know
    I am

23/06/22

Ways of writing

There are different
        ways of writing
These little
        missives

When
        Teri O'Neal
Came back
[As I knew she would]
They came
        all at once
In the night

And I lost the
        first one (forever)
Because I
        wasn't ready
Didn't have
        my little notebook and pen
                by my side

And it was only a
        question
Of whether I could
        scribble them down
                quickly enough
No question of
        editing / making changes

But now
        they are more

                reflective
Longer
Covering wider
        topics
Can be worked on
        revisited
                revised
Take more time

[I even make notes!]

                                        23/06/22

I heard

I heard you die

Or maybe I heard
     you
            just after
As the air left
     your body

It was the middle
     of the night
I guessed 2 or 3 a.m.
     but with hindsight
          it may have been earlier

I didn't put on the
     light
Didn't even really
     wake up
Thought you were
     snoring
Shoved you
     to get you
          onto your side
And went back to sleep

But it was the
     three sneezes
That puzzled me
And still do

[And Googling it
      hasn't helped]

25/06/22

That question again

How are you?

That question
       again
             and again

"Fine" I say
"Good"
And I am

But it is the new
       fine
The new
       good

All within narrow
       definitions
Narrowed circumstances

I am fine
I am good
      as me
          without you
Alone

With a huge
      gap
         in my life

That question?
Apparently it is

just a way
of saying
Hello

26/06/22

I veer

I veer   between
      talking
      to you
And
      talking
      about you

And back again

26/06/22

Up-to-date

I don't quite know how
            to update you
                        on the political situation

I don't even know
            if I should

You would be fascinated
            As am I
You would be horrified
            As am I

And you are no longer
            here
To explain it all
            to me
In constitutional
            terms
In an European / world history
            context

[And whoever thought Tiverton
            would be so
                        famous!]

26/06/22

Apricots

I saw some lovely
     apricots
In that nice
     greengrocers
And bought four
     to poach
     like you did

And had to find
     the recipe
You used to
     use

They were delicious
But did you sieve the syrup
To get rid of the bits of
     lemon peel?
I think I will
     next time

26/06/22

This volume

This volume (as it grows) has
a lot
of repetitions

The same issues
The same ideas
Revisited
reviewed
revised

Is that bad?

Not necessarily

Each time
I have progressed
a little
understood things
a bit more

Got further
down the track
along the lines
Of acceptance

And progress

And assimilation

And I think
the final entry

the last page
Will be on
the first
anniversary

26/06/22

Were you?

Were you
        tired?
Were you
        weary?
Were you
        weary
                of life?

A number of friends have
        commented
On this
One even said the
        thought you were
                "hollowed out"
But I think that that is
        going a bit
                too far
Overstating
        things

But
Your knees were bad
        making
                walking difficult
Your back was painful
        making
                writing your blog difficult
Your shoulder
        wasn't going
                to get better

You had had cancer
    survived
        been given the all clear
But there were
    after effects

As our doctor said
There were
    a lot of things wrong with you
        but all under control

So
    Were you tired?
    Were you weary?

27/06/22

Contacts

I have had contact
    with an unusual
        number of people
These last few days

Friday
    Saw working with a
        technician on the HiFi
    Going food shopping
        with a friend and
    then having tea
        with her

Saturday
    An old friend rang
Sunday
    A couple of people
        popped in
For a chat
    looked at my latest prints
        picked up some stuff

Then, in the evening,
    another old friend
    rang
And I had another
    long chat

This all leaves me
    tired
But

        energized
            stimulated

And led to these
        outpourings
Dated
        yesterday and
           today

                              27/06/22

Still no tears

Still no
      tears
But sometimes
      I wake up
In the middle
      of the night
And my eyes
      are wet
(as they are
      now)

30/06/22

Stage two revisited

These past few
        days
I have felt
        angry

Angry at
        the world
Angry at
        that question
Angry at
        myself
Angry at
        you

And I don't
        know why
Nothing
        has changed

03/07/22

"Your" handbag

I am using
     "your" handbag
          today

You were going to get
     one for me
          for my birthday
But we didn't
     get round to it

So I bought
     one
To use at
     your funeral
And
     your memorial
And it
     is lovely
And you
     would have loved it too

So thank you for my
     belated
          posthumous
Birthday
     present

[And a few days
     after I bought it
(and Yes it was expensive

      although maybe not in handbag terms)
They reduced it by
      30%
And then
      a few days later
By another
      20%

Ah well!]

03/07/22

What a week!

A week
 is a long time
  in politics
So they say
(Harold Wilson 1964?)

I have had to follow
 the news
  (avidly)
Without you

Without you
 to share it with
 to discuss it with

Without the
 insights of your
  specialist knowledge

It's been
 a lot
  of fun
And it isn't over yet

The Conservatives
 need to elect
  a new Leader
And
 thus
  the next Prime Minister
(again!)

There are umpteen
       runners
(unless they change the rules)

You would really
       be enjoying
          it
As am I
       but on my own
(so I have been
       texting people
to keep them
       up-to-date)

                                  07/07/22

I look back

I look back
At that part of
    my life
Between leaving husband
    number 2
(rebound from number 1
I don't talk about it)
And getting together
    with you

I don't
    regret that period
(despite all its
    awfulness)
and feel it was
    necessary

But have decided not
    to republish
The book
    of poetry
(the book you knew all about
but chose never to read)
Now that I have reread it
    in full
        straight through

Because
It says things people
    who know me now
        don't know about

And
It says things that
     didn't happen
          or I don't recognise
As being true
[Poetic licence?]

So let's let sleeping
     books
         lie

10/07/22

My face

My friend says she
    will never forget
        the look on my face
As they lowered you
    into the grave

She thinks that is when
    it hit me
When I knew it
    was real

But she couldn't see
    what I could
        see

The grave had been
    dug very deep
To allow for me
    to join you
        some day

[even though
    in fact
        as agreed
It will only be
    my ashes in a box]

And the water table
    in the cemetery
        is very high

So they were lowering
      you
Into
      water

That's what got me

They were lowering
     you
         into water

11/07/22

Talking about it

There are times
      when I am not sure
Any of it
      really happened

Think I have
      dreamt it
Think I am
      hallucinating

At those times
      talking about it
           going through that day
Bit by bit
Action by action
Helps a lot

I am sorry if it
      upsets
          you
the listener

12/07/22

Hello

Here I am updating
    you again
Re Pointless

Do you remember
    Rare Breeds of Poultry
As a Jackpot Round
    category?
It hung around for
    ages
Popping up every
    now and then
And Richard said that
    some-one should
        mug up on it

Well some-one did
And got through to the Final
And it came up

And their first two
    answers
Were
    incorrect
But the third one
    was right
        and pointless

[£2,750 since you ask]

15/07/22

118

There are problems in writing ...

There are problems in
      writing
Stuff
      that is
           autobiographical

No-one knows
      when you are
           using
Poetic licence

They assume everything
      you say is
Literally
True

Even when it
      isn't

Maybe there should be
      some way
           of flagging up the bits
You have taken
      licence with

19/07/22

Reading these

Every now and then
        I read some
                of these poems
Again
Maybe out loud

And find that
        some of them
I like
I think are good
I think are weak
I want to make
        changes to
                (and maybe do)
But above all
        I am pleased
If one makes
        me
                smile

19/07/22

When we bought this house ...

You always said
    "We will leave here
        in a box"
(Well, presumably, two)

So I had you brought
    home
(well OK outside
    in the hearse)
For just a few
    minutes

19/07/22

Why?

Is that it?
Is that why
      there's no drama
            no wailing
No tears?

I watch lots of
      rubbish TV
            crime dramas
And there's lots of
      noise
Lots of screaming
      & shouting
           & crying

But there was no drama
There were no doctors
There was no hope
      no expectation
            of recovery
Then denied

You made some noises
      in the night
I went back to
      sleep
You were peaceful
      you hadn't moved
When I woke up
      you were just
            dead

So maybe that
is why …

21/07/22

Your lawns

A while ago
       now
I had to make
       the decision
To let your lawns
       go brown

I know this will
       upset you
And you wouldn't
       have done the same

But we have had
       virtually
              no rain
This year

And now we have had
       a heatwave

There isn't a hosepipe
       ban
             yet
But there will be

I am not watering
       the garden
(or even my pots
       much)
If that is any
       consolation

So sorry
But the lawns
     will recover
As soon as
     we have some
          proper rain

[Although my pots might not!]

29/07/22

I've always said

I've always said there was
     a difference
Between
      loneliness and
         aloneness
And, up 'til now,
     (well last Sunday actually)
I have been alone
    but not
       lonely

On Sunday I was planning
      my Sunday dinner
(we always had a nice dinner
     on a Sunday)
Two potato croquettes
     (from the freezer)
A nice pork chop
     (from the freezer)
Frozen peas with
    shallots

Took the croquettes out
Couldn't find the pork chop
     (got really upset)
So had lamb (from the freezer)
    instead

And felt very
    very
      lonely

[Epilogue a few days later:
I have just gone
            into the freezer
To find some
            Indian snacks
                        for lunch today
And found the
            pork chop!
Maybe I'll have it
            this Sunday
With some potato rosti
            (from the freezer)]

29/07/22

They did it!

England won
        a major trophy
Do you believe that?
        (If you do
                you'll believe anything)

OK it was the
        European
Not the
        World
And the women
        not the men

Hang on
        that doesn't sound right

It was the
        WOMEN!

Football's come home
I am one
Of the thousands of
        young girls
Who loved playing
        football
(the only game I did
        like playing
Was any
        good at)

But was stopped

by the school
        by authority
(OK I only kicked the
       ball about
With the boys
      before school
          out of hours)
But still I was
      banned

But now ....
Still lots to do
But things really
      have changed

I have been watching
     a lot of it
        on TV

They really are very very
       good
It is how football
      used to be

Oh and the women's
      cricket team
Is very good
    too

Shame you have
      missed it all

31/07/22

Yet another drawer

I emptied
      another drawer
            the other day

(One of the little ones
      in the dressing table
            in the spare bedroom)

You know the one
      full of badges
            and the like

Most of the bits
      I took to the
            charity shop

Some I will keep

Some I threw away

But amongst it
      all
I found what I am
      pretty certain
            was your mother's
Wedding ring

I'll give that to
      your
            sister

Also two ESU
        badges
(I have someone
        in mind
                for those)

It's quite a challenge
        but quite fun
Finding the right
        home
                for things
I am quite enjoying
        it
But I can only do
        a bit
                at a time

It can get quite
        emotional
It can be quite
        tiring

[But also can be very rewarding
Mind you
        I have no idea
What to do with
        the cigar cutter!]

07/08/22

131

Dear Pat

You and I
        have never spoken
                have never met
(and
        maybe
                never will)

But we write
Often
At length

You say we are
        "anonymous"
And I know what
        you mean
But we aren't
        really
We each know
        who the other is
What our
        bond is
What ties
        us together

We can say anything
        about anything
To each other

Things we wouldn't
        couldn't
Say to our

closest friends
                    to family
And it helps

It helps
            both
                    of us

There was a point
            when I wondered
Maybe even
            worried
That writing to
            you
Was taking the
            place of
(Maybe even
            stopping me)
Doing this
Writing
            these poems

But NO
Quite the
            reverse

Our musings
Our ramblings
            inform these
                    works

Give me
            new topics
                    new ideas
To explore

So thank you

(and thank you for
          your support
                  your friendship)

07/08/22

Questions that need to be asked

Were you controlling?
    No
Was I submissive?
    No
Were you dominant?
    Yes
Was I passive?
    Yes
Was I happy?
    Yes
Were you?
    I think so
        I hope so

Does any of this
    matter
        now?
Yes

It helps me
    understand
It helps me
    move forward
To become
    me
        again
To become the
    new
        me

11/08/22

Burial or cremation?

I never wanted
          never believed in
             burial
Even from a very young
         age
It was always going to be
         cremation
             for me

You were a
         believer
Wanted a
         funeral
Wanted to be
         buried

We had an agreement

If you died first
There would be a
         funeral
The works
(I even threw in
         a memorial service
             for good measure)
And you would be
         buried
             in our plot

If I died first
You had my

permission
To arrange a
          funeral
And to bury
          me
                    in our plot

Now the first half
          is done
You are
          there

So, when I die,
          I will be
                    cremated
(no funeral, no fuss)
And
My ashes
          will be put into our plot
                    with you
All as agreed

However, I do
          wonder
Whether the reason
          I talk to you
                    like this
Address these poems
          to you
In the
          first person
Is because you
          still
                    physically
Exist

Because
      you weren't
            cremated

On the other hand
Maybe talking to you
Is just normal
Just how
      the survivor
            copes
Just how
     I
         cope

                              11/08/22

The visit (2)

We visited you
        today
Me and a
        friend

I hadn't been
        to see
                you
Since a few days
        after
                the funeral

Hadn't wanted to
(and it's not
        an easy journey
                by bus)

It felt very
        sad
It felt very
        odd
To think you were
        so close
Yet
        so far away

We scattered some
        yellow
                Freesias
(You will have
        a headstone

eventually)

And left you
there
again

14/08/22

Little things

A while ago
      (ten days, two weeks?)
I moved your
      soap dish and your
          soap
Away from the end of
      the bath
Away from the opposite corner
      to my own

After all this
      time
I suddenly realised
      it didn't need
          to be there

17/08/22

The visit (3)

During our visit
       the other day
I observed
       "It's very peaceful
          here"

"Yes"
       said my friend
"That's because
       they are
          all dead"

For some reason
       that cracked us
          both up
Couldn't stop
       laughing
Tears running
       down our faces

Hysteria
       I guess

A brief
       relief
A brief
       release
          from
The overriding
       sadness

19/08/22

3.20 a.m.

3.20 in the morning
Lying there
    awake
Eyes damp

"I can't do Christmas"

[Can't do
    the planning
        the (home-made) cards
    the presents
        the decorations

Any of it]

27/08/22

Another grief

I have tried
      to avoid
Writing about this
      in this
Your book

But you know
      about it
Know that I
      am grieving
Some-one else
      too

He died on
      V E Day
         2020

I hadn't seen
      hadn't spoken
         to him
Since 1972
Until he
      found me
         in 2017
One phone call
Some emails
      and
Then we broke off
      all contact
         again
That was what he

and his wife
    wanted
But you and I
    felt that it was
        unnecessary
But agreed to it
    provided
I would be told
He would be told
If one
    of us
        died

And that happened
    and the letters
        from his widow
Were lovely
She finally
    understood
Why he had found me
Why I needed to know
And you
    understood
That I had to
    grieve

I just didn't expect
    to be grieving
        you
Too

And now?
Now
    she and I
        have become

Email
       pals
Each other's
       bereavement
             counsellor

And I know
       you would be
             pleased

04/09/22

Someone to talk to

That's
         what
                  I miss
(amongst many other things)

Days go by
When I
         don't see
                  don't speak to
Anyone
(other than Bella the cat)

It's not just
         that I can't discuss
                  the day's news
         talk about
                  the sport
It's that I get
         out of practice

So when I do
         see someone
Or someone
         rings me
I can't
         stop
                  talking
I hold court
I "monologue"

I go over things

I must have
            told them before
(probably many times)

They can't get
        a word in
                edgeways
Then I feel guilty
        have to apologise

I really must try
        to get
                out more

                                05/09/22

Up-date

I was going
      to up-date you
            on the sport

(Graham Potter has gone
      to Chelsea
You always said
      that would happen
Even named
      the correct club)

But The Queen
      died

And now today
      is 9/11

                                11/09/22

Eating

You will be very
            pleased to know
(proud even)
That I am
            eating
                        properly
Like we did
Not
            like I did
                        when I lived alone before
Like I was doing
            when we met

It's not easy
So many things
            come in packs
                        for two
And some can't
            be frozen
And some can't
            be reheated
And even if they can
            you have to eat the same thing
                        twice

I have learnt
            to make
                        risotto
            to make
                        paella
but now have

            plain boiled rice
(can't do it the way you did)
You were always
        the rice cook

And I don't have
        a commis chef
And I don't have
        a "dustbox"
To eat up all the
        leftovers

And I have to eat
        on my own

                              11/09/22

The decision

A couple of weeks
After you died
I wrote:
(and I quote)

> "I always said
> That if you went first
> I would decide whether or not
> I wanted to continue"

And this idea would have applied
Whatever the reason was
For our no longer being together

That was over
      nine months ago

At that time
I also wrote:
> "Now that you have gone
> I can't make up my mind"

What I have found (so far)
    is that there
        is no decision to make
One just has to
    cope
Just get on with it
Take each day
    as it comes
And whatever

other
             cliché
One wishes to use

Anyway
Is there a decision
         to make
                  at all?

Suicide
         is
                  ultimately
Cowardly
Selfish

But also
         does it actually
                  exist?
Do we have
         that freedom?
         that choice?
Or is that act
         just an instrument
                  of Fate / of Destiny?

13/09/22

The next hurdle

The next hurdle?
      (well OK fence)
      Becher's Brook
            the first time round

Is the day
      after tomorrow

It would have been
      our wedding anniversary

I may make a pilgrimage:
Take a taxi
      to Warren Hill
and go to the
      Dew Pond
to your
      bench
and then
      walk
            home

20/09/22

Celebration / Remembrance

As I have said
>today is a special
>>day

And we used
>to make it
>>special

So I have tried
>to
>>too

Went up on
>the Downs

To the Dew Pond

To "your bench"

Took some flowers
>from the garden

Sat

Took some photos
>left the flowers

The weather was lovely

Walked back home

Will have a nice
>meal
>>this evening

The sort
>we would
>>have had

And I'll open
       one of the half bottles
                 of wine
You bought

And drink a little bit
       more than
                 usual
As we would
       have done

I feel
       I am doing
                 it right

22/09/22

I'm fine

I know I've said this
      before
But people keep
      asking me
            how I am
And I say
      "I'm fine"

But sometimes it all
      seems
            so surreal
That I am not sure
      if I
            have taken it all in
            have taken it in at all
Or if I just
      don't
            recognise
      don't
            acknowledge
      don't
            understand
What happened

That you are
      not
            just going to
come back
one day

22/09/22

157

When we bought this house (2)

When we bought
    this house
Thirteen years
    ago
You said it
    would be
Our last house

So we
    renovated it
    restored it
    redecorated it
        (in lovely Edwardian colours)
Did everything
Made it our own

We always said we had
    bought
"Four and a half
    newel post caps"
        (pewter, hand beaten, Glasgow School)
and "a view
    to die for …
Attached to
    a wreck"

And everyone agrees
    it is now
        a lovely house
And those views
    are breath-taking

So I am minded
         to stay
Why leave?
Where would I go?

25/09/22

You're fading

I have just
        realised
You are fading

Your image is
        becoming
                weaker
                paler
                sepia

But then
        suddenly
You are here
As real
        as if
                you
Are still
        with me

I guess
It is just
        my brain
Trying
        to cope

01/10/22

Repetition

I find myself
      repeating
            myself
In these
      scribblings

Looking at the
      same
            issues
Saying the
      same
            things

My excuse has been
      that I am
            exploring
New angles
New ideas

But I think that
      actually
            sometimes

I am just
      repeating
            myself

04/10/22

Last weekend

I had a
      weekend
          away
On an organised trip
      with lots of
          other people
Some of whom
      I / we have met
        before

But they didn't
      recognise
          me
What with your
      not being there
          with me
And with my hair
      being different

And I found it hard
To talk about
Anything else
Just told them
What had happened
And apologised

But they said
      it was good
That I could
      talk about it
Because that allowed

them to too
And there was
no embarrassment
no awkwardness
But I still
apologised

04/10/22

Getting there

At last
Finally
I've started
      feeling
            something

It is
As if I have
      woken up
As if I am
      coming out of a dream

I got cross
      the other day
Really
      angry

Then
(talking to the lady
      to try to sort out
            what to do
To mark the
      occasion
Of the anniversary
      of our lovely day
Followed by the anniversary
      of your death)
I got upset
Choked up
Nearly cried

And then
            talking to the friends
Who are
            going to join me
On those
            two days
I got all
            muddled
Couldn't
        think
                    straight
Couldn't
        talk
                    straight

I think that
        that
                is progress

06/10/22

At Last

I did it!
I cried

Not a lot and not for long but
    definitely
        proper crying

Standing there
Alongside
    your Best Man
    your old University friend
    your grave

(I had dug up
    some dandelions
You always hated
    dandelions)

We laid down
    some flowers
Talked to you
(Forgot to take
    a photo for others
        to see)

And then
I cried

It's been
    over ten months
    now

The same length
      of time
That other widows
      I know
Say it took
      them
To finally
      cry

Another step
      forward
Another step
      towards acceptance

R.I.P.

14/10/22

Rules

Rule number 1:
There are no rules

There is
No set way
        to grieve

Everyone has to
        do it
                    their own way
That is the
        most important thing
                    I have learned

And it has
        given me confidence
To just
        do it
However I feel
        day by day

16/10/22

Cyclamens

On that day
Your last day

We went cross
        country
Exeter to
        Henley-on-Thames
Via Stourhead
(and the Reading
        rush hour
            in the pouring rain)

At Stourhead they
        were getting a
            Christmas lightshow
ready

And we bought
        four
            Cyclamen
plants

Spent ages
        choosing them

In the summer
(during the drought)
They died down
(as cyclamens do)

Then three recovered

and one was about
to flower
But one had disappeared

Then
the other day
I noticed
It was growing
again
too
(albeit tiny but definitely there)

17/10/22

Just a scene

4.41 p.m.

I've just cried
    really really
        cried

Screamed
Shouted

I had been watching
    Wisting
        (Nordic noir)

I've recently gone
    back to
        the genre

Now I remember why
    I had stayed
        away

A character went into
    cardiac arrest
And they tried
    to save her
Failed

I know it is fiction
I know they are actors
But it seemed
    so real

But no-one knew
No-one tried to
     save
          you

Although they did
       try to save
            our cat sitter
And failed then
      too

24/10/22

I've been

I've been
    so
          resilient
(the doctor's word)
    so
          strong
    so
          focussed

Got a lot of
    things done

Has it all been
    just
          an act?

24/10/22

Earlier

I had
    a nasty fall
        earlier today

Hit
    my head
    my shoulder
    my arm
    my thigh

A lot of bruises
A lot of pain

So I have been
    resting
Not doing anything

Is that what
    let
        the other type of pain
in?

24/10/22

Little things (2)

It is
        the little things
                that
Catch you out

The other day
        I knocked
                one of the
Coffee cups
        out of the
                cupboard
And it
        smashed
                into smithereens

(You know
        the little stripey
                multi-coloured
Ones
        by
                Maxwell Williams
That we bought
        at an antiques fair
The ones you
        chose)

And it really
        upset
                me

30/10/22

175

Surrogate?

I have toothache
An infection
Raging

Last night I was
Holding my face
        screaming
                crying

Until the painkillers
        (and later the antibiotics)
Kicked in

A surrogate
        for the emotional
                and mental
Pain
        I feel?

03/11/22

The anniversary

THE ANNIVERSARY

     THE ANNIVERSARY

          THE ANNIVERSARY

Is soon
(less than three weeks)

And looms
     larger and
          larger

Dominates
     my thoughts

But really
     it is just
          another day

to get through

06/11/22

Locations

Apparently there are
        these codes
One for each
        square metre
        of the planet

One for
        our house / my house
        **** ****** *****

One for
        your bench
        ***** **** *****

One for
        where you are now
        ***** ***** *****

I didn't know about them
Did you?

                                    18/11/22

Coincidences (6)

I was having lunch
    with a friend
Sitting in her
    kitchen / eating area
Telling her about
    the arrangements
        for the anniversary
And just as I told her
    the name
        the location
Of the hotel
    where we are all
        meeting up
Staying
My phone rang

It was the hotel
Confirming
    the
        booking

19/11/22

The last first

A friend pointed out
       that
The anniversary
      will be
          the last first

After that
      every event
         (birthdays, anniversaries)
Will be
      the second time
         round

Will it get any
      easier?

[Epilogue:
Then I remembered the funeral; the memorial service
Those are yet to come]

21/11/22

Well a …

Well a
       year
Has now
       passed
Since
       you
             didn't wake up
But
      I
           did

                         24/11/22

Other books by Teri O'Neal

You are dead (but I am not ...) [or The Second Year]